A Soul's Journey

Poems by

Whitney Cason

Copyright © 2018 Whitney Cason

All rights reserved.

ISBN: 978-0-999106020
ISBN-13: 978-0-9991060-2-0

BIO.

A Soul's Journey is a collection of poetry built for the varied emotions of the heart and soul. This collection allows you to take a walk through a life who isn't perfect, and allows you the opportunity to identify with poetry that expresses when things are not always put together, or when everything feels like it's going just the way God intended.

A Soul's Journey tells the secrets you keep hidden deep inside and brings them to light, with hopes to promote support, encouragement and healing; and also acknowledge positivity and light with all the good things that the world brings us

Levitate

Take a minute and let your mind wander to the forbidden crevices of your brain;

The places you kept locked up, the deep dark spots you wanted to keep untouched.

The truth was too difficult to face, so you covered those places with lies to soften the blows.

You let the lies levitate over the truth, letting your emotions hover over what's really below the surface.

Are you willing to expose what lies beneath?

A NOTE

Some days, life is too much to bear.

The arguing to too much to hear.

The pain is too much to bear.

And I feel like ending it all could be a benefit to everyone involved.

Would you still care if I was gone?

Would life be easier now that your burden has left you?

Do you know if tears would fall at the thought of my non-existence?

I don't have to continue to stay around with someone or within something I cannot handle.

Sometimes all I want is to be free from the pain.

The Eye

What if beauty was in the eye of the beholder,

But the beholder was too broken to see it...

Would you be there to encourage her

To uplift her

To push her past those broken pieces to see the truth that lies within her spirit?

.

Gray

Within the space of like and lust,

Or hate and love.

Between together or apart,

Whether near or far.

Our existence is gray, not definite nor questionable.

Living in a constant state of confusion or uneasiness.

Playing mindless games of emotional tug-of-war with our hearts. Can the situation be any more gray?

Can our lives be anymore intertwined yet separate at the same time?

What's known is inevitable we cannot continue to live this way.

To suck the life out of one another by going back and forth, and back and forth.

Until the hurt fades away, until our path is a little more clear.

Or until we forget what we're even here for in the first place.

Years pass, we grow but not in sync.

How do you outgrow the person you were supposed to love forever?

Throwing Stone at Fragile Emotions

I can't let you continue to throw stones at my glass house and hide your hand like everything will be ok; it's not.

These walls, these walls of this glass house are crying. Tear-stained clear walls I've never seen so much transparent misery.

I'm a ticking time bomb inside these walls, and every day is another eggshell under your feet, my dear. Every day is another paranoid look over that shoulder; it's not ok.

I want to tell you that I'm ok but some days are the worst days and other days may be better days than some but most days are the shittiest days to come by.

So I just pray that I remember to be blessed that I even woke up that day, and that makes things a little better for that day.

You see, you shouldn't throw stones at a glass house and plant the evidence in the next man's hand.

Don't project that negative energy into another man's atmosphere when it doesn't belong there.

Don't allow me to place blame on a person who hasn't rightfully earned it

Beauty

It's hard to look at myself. It's hard to look at myself because I don't see what you do.

I see a withered and worn spirit, a hollow empty shell; somewhat less of myself.

You tell me, in so many ways and on so many days, that you see a beautiful soul and a flawless face; and I cringe as the words leave your lips.

I wonder "how can he be serious?" Does he even look in a mirror at me or is he only stealing glances and creating fantasies of who he wants me to be?

Does he truly see that my hair is always out of place, or that makeup never seems to make it to my face?

Does he see I'm not the size 9 I used to be, and have seemed to gained weight in areas and I'd rather hide behind my clothes?

I tend to be an introvert, I hide darkness behind a smile; and yet he still tells me I'm great to be around all the while.

I don't understand it, but he finds ways to make the darkest days bright for me.

Test

Standing at the edge of the earth.

Suffocating with thoughts surrounding an overwhelming life.

Begging for breath, praying for signs

That jumping to escape the wave is just as painful as enduring the wave

The mere difference is enduring the pain makes you stronger

Escaping the pain teaches you nothing.

Chasing my Pain

I wanted to find the answers to my problems in the bottom of this bottle,

But I realized that the only answers I'd gain would be hollow.

I knew this wasn't the way peace, but I took the road I traveled more often than not,

Instead of looking to more positive ways to cope with the loss,

I made a decision to be reckless, to think less of myself,

Then to expect the liquor to fill voids of stress and distress.

Like a needle being stuck into the pressure points of my neck,

This life can be harder to accept, when the reality has been something you come to expect.

I endure the pain, I embrace the agony, I suck it up and continue to push through.

Sometimes not knowing what to do, other times not having someone to turn to.

The world seems to close in on me; the walls in this room draw nearer and nearer.

My mind and my judgement being clouded, decisions are not nearly as clear.

The room constantly spinning; praying, dreaming, wishing and full of wonder.

Will things change, or will they remain the same? An undying question with and unknown answer.

If all things in the world require change,

Then why does the pain in my life remain constant?

Resurrected

What I once thought was a hollow hall that I couldn't find a way out of,

I found the light and it was good.

I found a way to resurrect happiness from the storms;

And create sunshine from the clouds.

In Case No One Ever Told You

You make the whole world beautiful; even amongst the ugliest of spaces.

Your presence shines a light on the darkest parts of reality.

You are the most unrealistic real thing to ever exist.

I want to dive into your heart, and erase every bad thing that's ever made it bleed.

Excuse my wayward approach to gathering your attention,

But I just needed you to know that your smile is like God's wildest intentions.

He made a beautiful masterpiece when he created you.

And I needed you to know that just how much that beauty is admired.

Love

I never knew I was in love with you until I was already waist deep;

Struggling without you there next to me to pull me up.

At first I buried it deep so the obvious wouldn't show, but it seemed through my pores like sweat on the hottest southern summer day.

I'm surprised you never noticed how deep this love ran for you....

Field Dreams

You want me to open to you,

Allow you to be one with my flesh,

Touch my soul with your essence

Yet.. there's still so much mystery to you.

Taking myself there with you,

Opening up to you

Like a field of flowers in full bloom

On the most beautiful April afternoon.

I await the day .....

The day where every morning feels like the perfect movie scene,

The day when your voice sings a melodious harmony with each moment we speak,

For our lives together to transcend beyond just an apprehensive walk into an idea called "us",

But until then,

I take pleasure in learning you,

Developing with you,

Evolving with you,

Until I can say that I'm fully aware and open to what this life could be with you.

A Love So Pure

I wonder if God made a mistake.

Did He really believe I was able to handle the amount of love I have for you in this lifetime?

Because my one fear in this world is that I won't have enough time..

I won't have enough time to give you every ounce of the love I have for you in this lifetime.

I only pray that I tell you I love you enough.

I hope that I hug you enough,

That I give you enough kisses,

That I make you laugh enough.

And even if I gave you enough of all of these things to last five lifetimes, I would still feel like I need to do it all just one more time for good measure.

I don't know if there's enough love to go around after you've stolen my heart.

As I watch you, even when you don't notice me watching you.

Praying that you know that I'll always love more than my soul could possibly take.

Mirror

Today, I looked in the mirror.
I stood there longer than I ever had before.
Longer than it took to exfoliate, cleanse and moisturize,
Longer than it took to brush my teeth;
Even longer than it took to make myself look mediocre for the day of work ahead.
Today, I looked beyond just seeing a face.
Today, I painted a picture.
I envisioned a life much different from what's currently unfolding.
I saw myself full of laughter, vibrant and pure.
Taking chances and making valuable mistakes that upgrade to life lessons.
I took a leap and didn't care if I fell flat on my face.
I hugged more of my loved ones, and told them the things you never want to wait until the next day to say,
Because with none of us is a new day promised, so you must take the opportunity to shed light on your thoughts, especially to those whom you cherish the most.
I confessed the sins and shed the weight of my world, because bearing the truth opens the soul and lets forgiveness in.
I prayed, I asked God not to make me perfect, but to make me someone that others could be proud of;
An imperfect human with flaws, but the ability to recognize and make amends.
I left all of what and who I wronged in the vision of my mirror.
And after I left the mirror, I started to get it right.

Vulnerable

Open;

Unapologetic, without regard to the outside world's opinion

Honest;

A need to release life's burdensome troubles from across your shoulders...

I yearn to be vulnerable but I don't want to show weakness;

I fear that you'll see my holes in my thick skin.

I know there's a place for those emotions here,

You do all these things to me, knowing at some point I'll succumb to your advances.

You know that even though you ruined me, there's a piece of my heart that you know you still belong in.

You know I have a problem and all you do is feed the flame.

I'm addicted to the worst drug of its kind; loving a man who doesn't deserve the pleasure of loving all of me, and you don't mind being my dealer.

A Want

If there was ever a space, a moment or a time to be enveloped in your essence;

I'd be addicted to the idea of being a prisoner to your love.

I want to lay around doing nothing, but feeling everything with you.

I could find a million ways to say I love you,

But it gives me goosebumps for me to only hear you say "I love you too."

0%

I looked at photos of you while singing along to love songs until my phone died.

I think that's when I knew true love was a tangible thing.

I'm Sorry

I don't know anything more than to write down the words that pour out of my soul,

Like a waterfall of tears after you left me that cold morning in November.

I watched you throw your clothes in a trash bag because you were so mad you couldn't ask me where the suitcase was.

I didn't mean to hurt you….

I know as a man you were taught not to cry but I'll admit I died inside when I saw that tear roll down your cheek like a devastating avalanche ready to demolish the small town that sits below it.

I'll say it again, I didn't mean to hurt you. All I wanted was to lie to you but I knew honesty was the best policy so I took a leap and told the truth no matter how much I knew it would damage you.

I knew the scars of my truth would be the devastation of our legacy; but I couldn't live with the thought of building a future of lies between us.

Perfectly Imperfect

I strive for perfection,

But sometimes almost doesn't count.

And these imperfect qualities are all I have to give,

99% is sometimes all I can muster, and that 1% just won't come to pass

I know your expectations of me are higher because my title demands it,

But I can only provide so much of myself before my soul begins to cry out from the exhaustion of trying so hard to be "perfect"

This perfection you seek is in the eye of the beholder,

In God's eye, I am wonderfully made, and purely perfect;

However, in yours I always seem to need improvement, and my best is never enough.

Suicidal Silence

Sometimes I keep music blaring because the silence feels like suicide.

Or maybe I use the music to replace the empty feeling you left in my life.

I don't hear your voice anymore; the calm before a storm,

So now I play the music so loud that I hope my eardrums bleed.

Kind of like the tears I cried the day you left my world silent, like a pin dropping in a dark room.

Knee Deep

I hadn't spent time knee deep in the thought of loving you in a while,

because nowadays it's more like being knee deep in the agonizing,

painstaking reality of living without you.

I can only be as strong as my heart can take.

Your love is synonymous with pain; the kind of pain that's unhealthy, yet to addictive to let go of.

I want to let you go, but there are things about you that keep me stuck.

My mind knows what needs to be said in order to leave,

But my heart aches whenever I stay.

Blessing

Sometimes the half empty smile

Is all I could muster from chiseling away at

the pain that lay across my face.

....

Intentional

What is life without purpose?

I wake up every morning telling the world i will be something.

I try to remind myself that with every challenge the world brings, it is my job to rise above it all.

"Set intentions, and be intentional" is an affirmation I look at every morning to remind myself to be something, do something and to make every moment in life matter.

What is life without intentions? What is living without a purpose?

Falling

Save me.

Protect me.

Embrace me.

Comfort me.

Catch me before I end up falling out of love with you.

I'm begging because I'm not ready to give up the fight.

I don't want our light to dim so quickly.

But if you don't grab me up, I fear our ending will be a tragedy.

Satisfaction

In all the facets of this world,

I find solace in your embrace.

I find contentment in who you are,

There's not much more I need to sustain this feeling.

If you could always just be this amazing,

That is enough for me.

#QUEEN

Naturally nappy loc'd from root to tip or curls flying to and fro from an afro as tall as her confidence is

Skin tone the color of freshly preserved blackberry jam

Her scent a mixture of shea butter and coconut oil;

Body made of twists and turns, shifts and curves, thicker than buttermilk biscuits and sweeter than honey;

She was original.

She is Queen.

Attitude sharp like a blade,

Wit as quick that cracked like a whip;

She could cut you with her eyes, or even kill you with kindness;

But she never had to show how down she really was,

Unless someone pushed her to the limit with their degrading level of ignorance,

She knew how to speak with a tone that could make the tallest mountain move, yet still sound as feminine as ever,

Clever, never wavering in her confidence or wary in her love of self;

A lover of all things melanin and woke to the bullshit you may try to pull over on her,

She is Queen.

Knowledge on 100,

Finer than aged wine,

She didn't need the validation of a man to tell her what was already known;

Her legacy was flawlessly made,

Her future bright and abundantly clear,

Loyal to a fault and beyond deserving of her royal title;

Personified she is, untouchable she will remain, dignified in her appearance and snatched in her frame;

She is Queen, a Queen is She.

ABOUT THE AUTHOR

Whitney Cason is an author and part-time blogger. She currently works in the field of social work and has a background in criminal justice and sociology from Valdosta State University. She has been writing for years in the genre of poetry and fiction short stories. Her most recent publications are *From a Lover's Mouth* and her first-published fiction novel, *Playing with Fire*. She currently is the owner and organizer of her own publishing start-up, Writing in Color Publishing, LLC.

Made in the USA
Columbia, SC
31 July 2024